Eve Fehilly

Great Singer Songwriters

CW01080461

Wise Publications
part of The Music Sales Group
London/New York/Paris/Sydney/Copenhagen/Berlin/Madrid/Tokyo

Published by
Wise Publications
8/9 Frith Street, London W1D 3JB, UK.

Exclusive Distributors:

Music Sales Limited
Distribution Centre, Newmarket Road, Bury St Edmunds, Suffolk IP33 3YB, UK.

Music Sales Pty Limited
120 Rothschild Avenue, Rosebery, NSW 2018, Australia.

Order No. AM984775
ISBN 1-84609-338-4
This book © Copyright 2006 Wise Publications,
a division of Music Sales Limited.

Music arranged by Jack Long
Music processed by Paul Ewers Music Design
Compiled by Nick Crispin
Cover Photos (left to right): Bob Dylan (LFI), David Bowie (LFI),
Jackson Browne (Henry Diltz/Corbis), David Gray (Miriam Santos-Kayda/Retna),
John Lennon (Harry Goodwin) and Paul McCartney (Mick Hutson/Redferns)
Printed in the EU

Also available:
Great Singer-Songwriters: Female Edition
Twenty-two self-penned classics arranged for piano, voice and guitar, including
Angel (Aretha Franklin), A Case Of You (Joni Mitchell), Jolene (Dolly Parton),
Other Side Of The World (KT Tunstall), Silent All These Years (Tori Amos),
Uninvited (Alanis Morissette), Why (Annie Lennox) and You're So Vain (Carly Simon).
Order No. AM984753

Your Guarantee of Quality
As publishers, we strive to produce every book to the highest commercial standards.
This book has been carefully designed to minimise awkward page turns and to make
playing from it a real pleasure.

Particular care has been given to specifying acid-free, neutral-sized paper made from
pulps which have not been elemental chlorine bleached. This pulp is from farmed
sustainable forests and was produced with special regard for the environment.

Throughout, the printing and binding have been planned to ensure a sturdy, attractive
publication which should give years of enjoyment.

If your copy fails to meet our high standards, please inform us and we will gladly
replace it.

www.musicsales.com

Ain't No Sunshine

Words & Music by Bill Withers

4

Brown Eyed Girl

Words & Music by Van Morrison

1. Hey where did we go days__ when the rains__
2. What-ev-er hap-pened to Tues-day and so__
3. So hard to find my way now__ that I'm all__

__ came, down__ in the hol-low,
__ slow, go-ing__ down the old mine,
__ on my own. I saw you just the oth-er day,

Blind Willie McTell

Words & Music by Bob Dylan

11

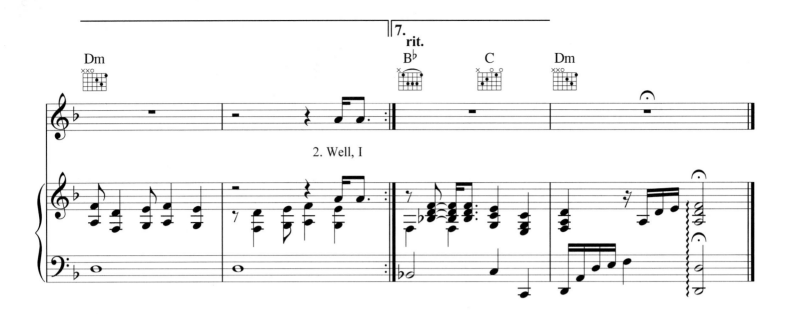

2. Well, I

Verse 2:
Well, I heard the hoot owl singing
As they were taking down the tents
The stars above the barren trees
Were his only audience
Them charcoal gypsy maidens
Can strut their feathers well
But nobody can sing the blues
Like Blind Willie McTell.

Verse 3:
See them big plantations burning
Hear the cracking of the whips
Smell that sweet magnolia blooming
See the ghosts of slavery ships
I can hear them tribes a-moaning
Hear the undertaker's bell
Nobody can sing the blues
Like Blind Willie McTell.

Verse 4:
There's a woman by the river
With some fine young handsome man
He's dressed up like a squire
Bootleg whiskey in his hand
There's a chain gang on the highway
I can hear them rebels yell
And I know no one can sing the blues
Like Blind Willie McTell.

Verse 5:
Instrumental (until *)

𝄋 *Verse 6:*
Well, God is in heaven
And we all want what's His
But power and greed and corruptible seed
Seem to be all that there is
I'm gazing out the window
Of the St. James Hotel
And I know no one can sing the blues
Like Blind Willie McTell.

Verse 7:
Instrumental

12

Come Pick Me Up

Words & Music by Ryan Adams & Van Alston

Did I Dream (Song To A Siren)

Words & Music by Tim Buckley & Larry Beckett

Gm   F

Here I am,   here I am,_____   wait - ing to
O my heart,   O my heart_____   shies from the
Here I am,   here I am,_____   wait - ing to

1.   2.
E♭   E♭   Gm

hold   you."____   sor - row._____

3.
E♭   Gm

hold_____   you."____

Goodbye Yellow Brick Road

Words & Music by Elton John & Bernie Taupin

Moderately (Swung ♪'s)

1. When are you gon-na come down, when are you going to land?___ I
(Verse 2 see block lyric)

should have stayed___ on the farm,___ should have list-ened to my___ old man.___ You

know you can't hold me for-ev - er, I did-n't sign up with you. I'm

not a pre - sent for your friends to o - pen, this boy's too young to be sing-ing the

blues. Ah.

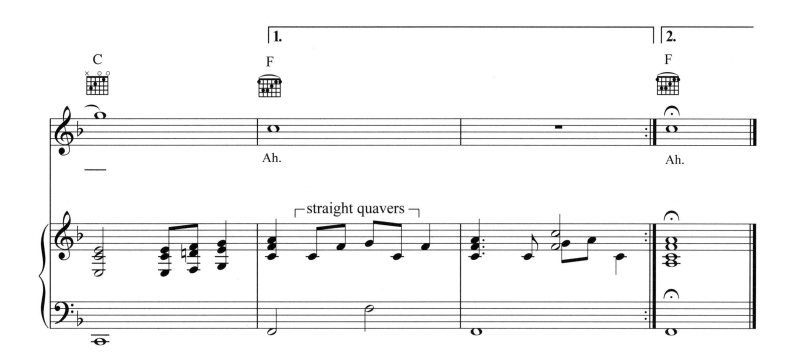

Verse 2:

What do you think you'll do then?
I bet that'll shoot down your plane.
It'll take you a couple of vodka and tonics
To set you on your feet again.
Maybe you'll get a replacement,
There's plenty like me to be found.
Mongrels who ain't got a penny
Singing for titbits like you on the ground.
Ah, ah.

So goodbye yellow brick road, *etc.*

Funny How Time Slips Away

Words & Music by Willie Nelson

1. Well hel-

-lo there, my, it's beeen a long, long time.
new love, I hope that he's do-in' fine.
go now, guess I'll see you a - round.

"How'm I do - in?" Oh, I guess that I'm do-in'
Heard you told him that you'd love him till the end of
Don't know when though, nev - er know when I'll be back in

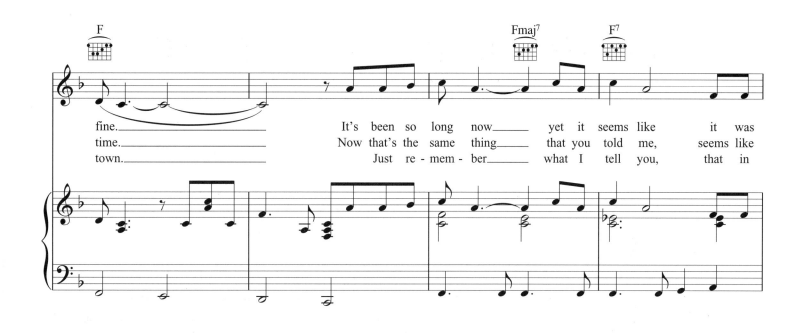

fine. _____ It's been so long now _____ yet it seems like it was
time. _____ Now that's the same thing _____ that you told me, seems like
town. _____ Just re - mem - ber _____ what I tell you, that in

on - ly yes - ter - day. _____ Ain't it fun - ny _____ how time slips a -
on - ly yes - ter - day. _____ Ain't it fun - ny _____ how time slips a -
time _____ you're gon - na pay. _____ And it's sur - pris - ing _____ how time slips a -

- way. _____ 2. How's your
- way. _____ 3. Got - ta - way. _____

27

Have A Little Faith In Me

Words & Music by John Hiatt

Hallelujah

Words & Music by Leonard Cohen

Verse 3:
You say I took the name in vain
I don't even know the name
But if I did, well really, what's it to you?
There's a blaze of light in every word
It doesn't matter which you heard
The holy or the broken Hallelujah.

Hallelujah *etc.*

Verse 4:
I did my best, it wasn't much
I couldn't feel, so I tried to touch
I've told the truth, I didn't come to fool you.
And even though it all went wrong
I'll stand before the Lord of Song
With nothing on my tongue but Hallelujah.

Hallelujah *etc.*

I Walk The Line

Words & Music by Johnny Cash

Mmm.

1. I keep a close watch on this heart of mine. I keep my eyes wide op-en all the time. I keep the

ends out for the tie that binds, be - cause you're

mine, I walk the line.

Mmm.

2. I find it
4. You've got a

Mmm.

3. As sure as

night is dark and day is light. I keep you

on my mind both day and night. And hap-pi-

43

Kooks

Words & Music by David Bowie

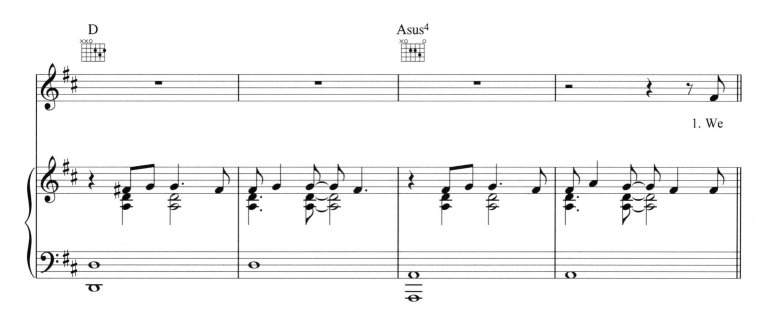

bought a lot of things___ to keep you warm and dry,___ and a

2. And if you ev - er have__ to go to school,___ re -

fun - ny old crib___ on which the paint won't dry.___

-mem - ber how they messed up this old fool!___

I bought you a pair___ of shoes,___ a

Don't pick fights with the bul-lies or the cads,___ 'cause I'm

Landed

Words & Music by Ben Folds

Con pedale

50

leave my-self_ be - hind, and I've been fly-ing high_ all_ night._

So come pick_ me_ up, I've land - ed.

52

2. The dai - ly dra - mas___ she made from no - thing,___

so no-thing ev - er made_ them right.___ She liked to push me___

and talk me back_ down till I be - lieved__ I was the cra - zy one, and

53

in a way__ I guess__ I was.. But I op-ened my eyes__ and walked out__ the door and the

clouds came tum - bl - ing down,__ and it's "bye bye.___ Good - bye,__ I___ tried."__

Tread - ing the sea__ of her trou - bled mind had to
2° Down comes the__ reign of the te - le - phone czar,

To Coda ✛

leave my - self be - hind__ sing - ing "bye bye.___ Good - bye,__ I___ tried."__
it's O. K. to call__ and I will an - swer__ for my - self.

54

I've come a - lone.

It's ov - er.

D.S. al Coda

But I

56

Come pick__ me up._____ Vocal ad lib.

Come pick__ me up.____

I've land - ed.____

Lawyers, Guns And Money

Words & Music by Warren Zevon

went home with a wait-ress, the way I al-ways do;

how was I___ to know___ she was

with the Rus - sians too?

I was gam-bling in___ Ha-va - na;

I took a lit - tle risk. Send

59

Send law-yers, guns and mo-ney; the

shit has hit the fan!

Repeat to fade

Send law-yers, guns and mo-ney.

62

Lost Cause

Words & Music by Beck Hansen

1. Your sor - ry eyes   that cut through bone,
2. There's too ma-ny peo - ple   you used to know;

67

Lover, You Should've Come Over

Words & Music by Jeff Buckley

feels like he should be___ hav-ing his fun.___ And much too blind to see (the) da-mage he's

done. And some-times a man must a - wake to find that real-ly he has no___ one.___

_____ So I'll wait for you,___ and I'll burn. Will I ev-er see your

___sweet re turn? Oh, will I ev-er learn? Oh, oh,___ lov-er, you should-'ve come

71

deaf, dumb and blind to see the damage I've done.

oh,   ah,   ah,   lov - er,   you should've come_____

Sweet lov - er,   you should've come_____

1, 2.

ov - er.____
ov - er.____

Yeah, yeah, yes.
Oh, love, but I've waited for you.

3.

ov - er.____

dim.

It's not too late.____

rit.

p

Verse 3   Lonely is the room, the bed is made
The open window lets the rain in
Burning in the corner is the only one
Who dreams he had you with him

Northern Sky

Words & Music by Nick Drake

1, 4. I ne - ver felt ma - gic cra - zy as this,
(Verses 2 & 3 see block lyric)

I ne - ver saw moons knew the mean - ing of the sea.

76

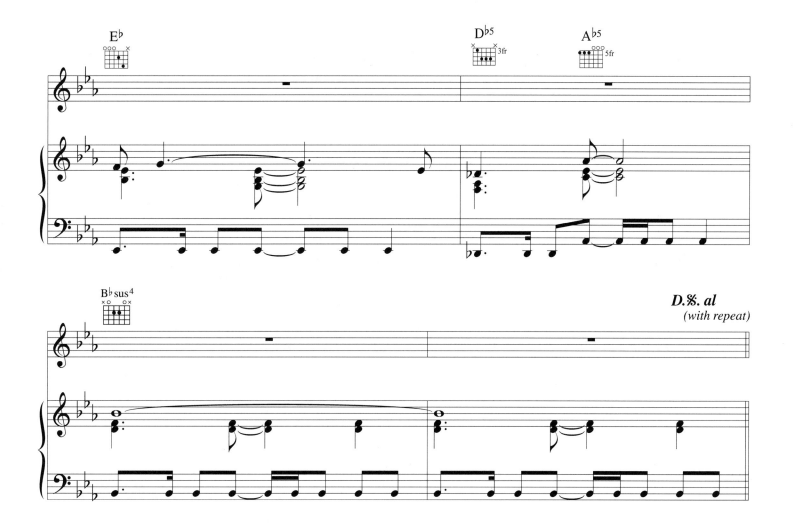

Verse 2:
I've been a long time that I'm waiting
Been a long time that I've blown
I've been a long time that I've wandered
Through the people I have known
Oh, if you would and you could
Straighten my new mind's eye.

Verse 3:
Would you love me for my money
Would you love me for my head
Would you love me through the winter
Would you love me till I'm dead
Oh, if you would and you could
Come blow your horn on high.

The Pretender

Words & Music by Jackson Browne

cool of the ev-'ning strolls_____ The Pre-ten-der._____
there? Say a prayer for The Pre-ten-der,_____

He knows that all his hopes_ and dreams_____ be-gin and
who start-ed out so young_ and strong,_____ on-ly to sur-ren-der._

end there._

(Ah, the laugh-ter) of the lov-ers as they run through the night,_____

83

Sail Away

Words & Music by David Gray

Sail a-way— with me, ho-ney, I put my heart— in your hands.

Sail a-way— with me ho-ney now,— now,— now.—

and ev - ’ry - thing _____ I held _____ so dear _____

dis - ap - peared _____ with - out a trace. _____

2. Though all the times _____ I tast - ed love, _____
(Verse 3 see block lyric)

nev - er knew _____ quite _____ what I had. _____

Sail a - way with me ho - ney now, now, now.

sail a - way with me; what will be will be.

1. I wan-na hold you now, now, now.

2. now, now.

Sail a - way with me, ho - ney, I put my heart in your hands.
(Choruses 5, 6 & 7 see block lyric)

88

Verse 3:
I've been talking drunken gibberish
Falling in and out of bars
Trying to get some explanation here
For the way some people are.
How did it ever come so far?

Chorus 5:
Sail away with me, honey
I put my heart in your hands.
It breaks me up if you pull me down, woh.
Sail away with me; what will be will be.
I wanna hold you now, now, now.

Chorus 6 & 7:
(Whistle)

Sea Song

Words & Music by Robert Wyatt

A Song For You

Words & Music by Gram Parsons & Chris Hillman

and to - mor - row__ we will still__ be_____ there._____

Violin

And to - mor - row   we may still___ be___ there.___

Steppin' Out

Words & Music by Joe Jackson

-ty   so   fine.___   Look, and dry___ your eyes.___
car   and   drive___   to the oth - er side.___

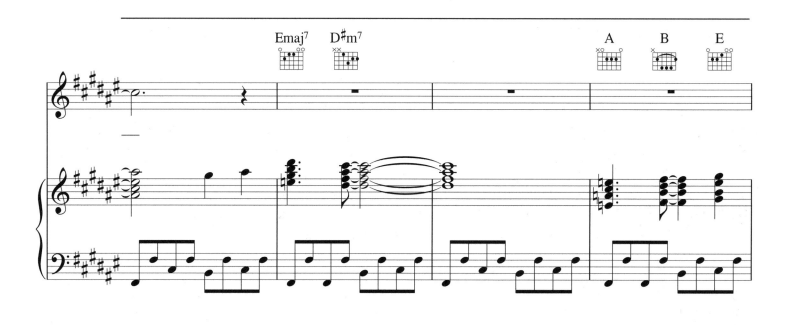

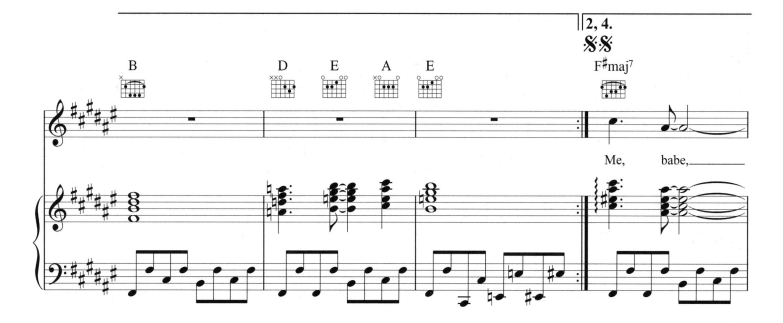

Me,   babe,___

103

Verse 3:
We are young but getting old before our time
We'll leave the TV and the radio behind
Don't you wonder what we'll find
Steppin' out tonight?

Verse 4:
You can dress in pink and blue just like a child
And in a yellow taxi turn to me and smile
We'll be there in just a while
If you follow me.

Stuck On You

Words & Music by Lionel Richie

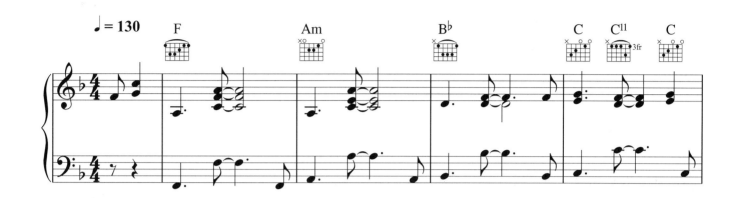

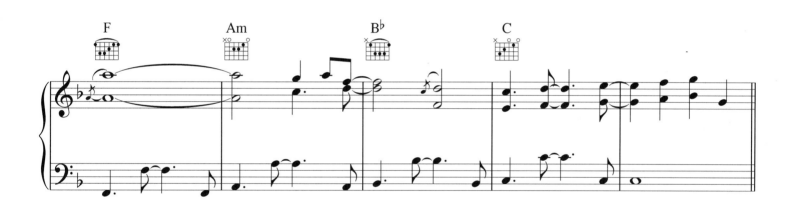

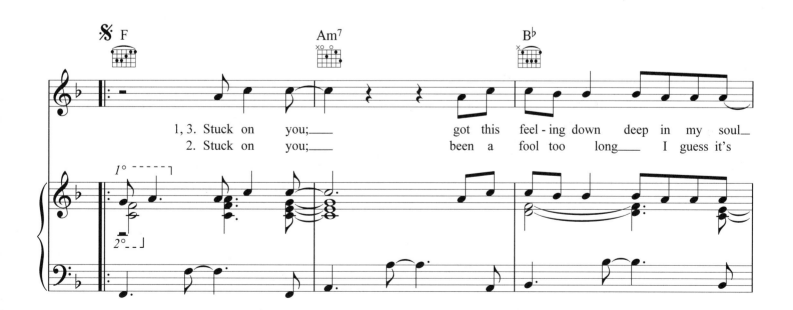

1, 3. Stuck on you;___ got this feel-ing down deep in my soul___

2. Stuck on you;___ been a fool too long___ I guess it's

might - y glad you stayed.____
might - y glad you stayed.____

Oh, I'm leav - ing on____ that mid -

Waltz #2 (XO)

Words & Music by Elliott Smith

Watching The Wheels

Words & Music by John Lennon

I just had to let it go.____

I just had to____ let it go.____

I just had to____ let it go.____

119

Waterfalls

Words & Music by Paul McCartney

I need love like a rain-drop needs a show-er, like a se-cond needs the hour ev-'ry min-ute of the day and it would-n't be the same if you ev-er should de-cide to go a-way. Don't go jump-ing wa-ter-falls please keep to the lake.

poco rit.

rit. molto

You Do Something To Me

Words & Music by Paul Weller

won - der - ful

(Verse 3: instrumental to chorus)

then chase it all a - way,

mix - ing my e - mo -

- tions, that throws me back a - gain.

CHORUS

Hang - ing on the

124

to, _____ just close e - nough _____ to tell you that: _____

You do _____ some - thing to me, _____

some - thing deep in - side. _____

123456789